Sandra Markon

Books by Eva Deutsch Costabel

New England Village
The Pennsylvania Dutch

THE JEWS OF NEW AMSTERDAM

Written and illustrated by
Eva Deutsch Costabel

ATHENEUM   New York   1988

*I dedicate this book to the state of Israel and its people; also to
my grandnieces and grandnephews born there: David, Liat, Avital,
Daniel, Yonathan, and Michal.*

*Many thanks to Rabbi Malcolm H. Stern, president of the Jewish Historical
Society of New York, for taking the time to check the manuscript and
for his valuable advice.*

———————————

Library of Congress Cataloging-in-Publication Data

Costabel, Eva Deutsch.
The Jews of New Amsterdam/written and illustrated by Eva Deutsch
Costabel.—1st ed.
p.   cm.
Bibliography: p.
Summary: Traces the events leading to the arrival of the first
group of Jews in the Dutch colony of New Amsterdam in 1654 and
describes how they adapted and eventually prospered under Dutch, and
later British, rule.
ISBN 0-689-31351-9
1. Jews—New York (N.Y.)—History—17th century—Juvenile
literature.   2. New York (N.Y.)—Ethnic relations—Juvenile
literature.   3. New York (N.Y.)—History—Colonial period, ca.
1600–1775—Juvenile literature.   [1. Jews—New York (N.Y.)—
History—17th century.   2. New York (N.Y.)—History—Colonial
period, ca. 1600–1775.]   I. Title.
F128.9.J5C73 1988
974.7′1004924—dc19
87-27873   CIP   AC

*The title page scene is based on the cyclorama at
the Museum of the City of New York.*

Atheneum
Macmillan Publishing Company
866 Third Avenue, New York, NY 10022
Collier Macmillan Canada, Inc.
Type set by Linoprint Composition, New York City
Printed in U.S.A.
Typography by Mary Ahern
First Edition

10 9 8 7 6 5 4 3 2 1

Contents

Introduction

I have been fascinated with American history and with the stories of the people of many nations who built this country. Many came here—because of persecution, poverty, and wars—to find a haven and a better future.

This book deals with the early history of the Jews of New Amsterdam. It is a story of the hope, courage, and perseverance of a people who had to adjust to a new life in the New World. Jewish history is complicated and often painful—a story of overcoming and renewal and, ultimately, great contributions to a new land.

Since I, too, am an immigrant to this great land, their story is also my story, but even more, it is a testament to the greatness of the human spirit.

I was very touched by the poem "The Jewish Cemetery at Newport," written by Henry Wadsworth Longfellow. He said it better than I could:

How strange it seems! These Hebrews in their graves,
  Close by the street of this fair seaport town,
Silent beside the never-silent waves,
  At rest in all this moving up and down!

And these sepulchral stones, so old and brown,
  That pave with level flags their burial-place,
Seem like the tablets of the Law, thrown down
  And broken by Moses at the mountain's base.

The very names recorded here are strange,
  Of foreign accent, and of different climes;
Alvares and Rivera interchange
  With Abraham and Jacob of old times.

How they came here? What burst of Christian hate,
  What persecution, merciless and blind,
Drove o'er the sea—that desert desolate—
  These Ishmaels and Hagars of mankind?

Pride and humiliation hand in hand
  Walked with them through the world where'er they went;
Trampled and beaten were they as the sand,
  And yet unshaken as the continent.

The Inquisition

A tradition as old as the Bible tells us that Jews were living in Spain in ancient times. When Germans subdued the Romans, they found the Jews in Spain civilized and enlightened. They were farmers, dyers, glass-makers, and traders.

In A.D. 711, new invaders—the Moors, Moslems from North Africa—arrived. They were an educated people, who shared their knowledge and made Spain a cultural center. During this period, the Jews developed their poetry and philosophy, and studied astronomy (vital to navigation) and medical science. They built synagogues and academies, served as advisers to Moslem leaders, and sent trading ships to the Orient.

However, in other European countries Jews were being persecuted by the Christian leaders, exploited by taxation, and falsely accused of all sorts of crimes. Gradually, the Christians reconquered Spain, and by 1250, northern Spain was free of Moorish rule.

At first the life of the Jews was unaltered; their prosperity continued and so did their freedom.

In the late 1300s, in the Christian parts of Spain, church leaders debated religion with rabbis. Often the rabbis' arguments were successful, and jealous priests aroused the mobs, and many Jews were forced to become Christians. Many of the new Christians—the Spanish called them "Marranos" ("pigs," because they would not eat pork)—were still practicing Jewish customs, but some Marranos even became courtiers.

The Spanish rulers enacted new religious laws based on "purity of blood," not on faith alone. King Ferdinand and Queen Isabella allowed the Catholic Church to bring in the Inquisition, a court to try those who disobeyed Church laws.

Torquemada, the chief inquisitor and the queen's priest, established his power by promoting the hatred and suspicion created by the laws. The war with the Moors was very expensive and the royal treasury was almost empty. The Marranos, who were rich and powerful, were accused of not being faithful Christians. Thousands were tortured and burned at the stake, and their immense wealth was confiscated by the Inquisition to fill the royal treasury again.

Torquemada also convinced the queen that exiling Jews would help unite the country. So, in 1492, King Ferdinand and Queen Isabella proclaimed the Edict of Expulsion and the Jews were given four months to get out of the country, leaving behind all their possessions and all that they had accomplished for centuries. Some of the enormous wealth acquired by Spain from the exiled Jews helped to finance Columbus's voyages to the New World.

Jews in Brazil

Many Spanish Jews, called Sephardim, fled to neighboring Portugal, where King John required only that they help pay taxes in return for permission to stay. But the daughter of Ferdinand and Isabella, betrothed to King John's son Manuel, refused to marry him until the "infidel" Jews were banished from Portugal as well.

Manuel wanted to keep the Jews, so, in 1497, he ordered his soldiers to kidnap all the Jewish children and have them baptized and gave their parents the choice of becoming Christian or being exiled.

Even before this event, Portuguese Jews had ventured into Brazil. In 1500, Fernando de Loronha, a Marrano buccaneer, had explored the tropical wilderness of the Brazilian coast with five ships, and had claimed the coast for Portugal. By 1503, the first fortress on the coast was built.

For about a century and a half, Jewish communities enjoyed freedom in Brazil, developing commerce, both in importing and exporting. They started sugar and tobacco plantations and were the first to grow the coffee and tea so much in demand in Europe.

In 1630, the Dutch captured the colony at Recife and the Jews there prospered under Dutch rule as merchants and financiers. In 1654, the Portuguese recaptured Recife, and the Dutch and the Jews who had fought with them were given three months to leave the colony.

Jews Arrive in New Amsterdam

In 1654, Jacob Barsimson, a Sephardi from Holland, arrived in New Amsterdam. Governor Peter Stuyvesant wanted only Dutch Reformed Christians in his colony, but since he had money and a passport giving him the right to live in the colony, Jacob Barsimson was allowed to stay.

Then, early on a September morning in 1654, a French vessel, the *Sainte Catherine,* sailed into New Amsterdam harbor from the West Indies bringing twenty-three poor, tired Jews from Recife, Brazil.

These Jews came from the Dutch colony that had been recaptured by the Portuguese. They had tried to join other Portuguese Jews who had established a community in Amsterdam. Shipwrecked in a storm, they were picked up by the French ship. It was going to Canada, but the Captain, Jacques de la Motthe, agreed to take them and other Dutch from Brazil to New Amsterdam.

Captain de la Motthe

The Jews, used to wealth and a fine life-style, regarded New Amsterdam, with its seven hundred and fifty inhabitants, as a godforsaken place.

The arrival of a vessel from abroad was a great event for the Dutch colonists, who were expecting letters and news from the mother country and merchandise they needed for their daily life. Native Americans also flocked to the incoming boat to barter their furs. Neither group was pleased to see penniless foreigners sail into the harbor.

Captain de la Motthe wasn't pleased, either, because he had only received 930 guilders from his passengers, who had hoped to borrow money from their families and friends in Holland to pay the rest. The last meager possessions of the Jews were put on auction to pay de la Motthe. The kindly Dutch bought the items; still, the amount raised was not enough, so Moses Ambrosius and David Israel were taken to jail.

Governor Stuyvesant's Request

Governor Peter Stuyvesant was not happy to have a group of poor Jews from Brazil in his colony and promptly wrote to his employers, the Dutch West India Company, asking permission to expel them. Quakers, Baptists, Lutherans, and Presbyterians were not welcome either.

What Stuyvesant did not realize was that the Dutch West India Company had Jewish stockholders. The refugees immediately wrote to family and friends in Holland about their treatment in New Amsterdam, and these Sephardim of Amsterdam petitioned the Dutch West India Company to let the Jews stay in New Amsterdam, pointing out that experienced merchants would make useful and productive settlers in the colony.

In the spring of 1655, exactly seven months after the Jews had sailed into New Amsterdam harbor, the flag on top of the fort announced the arrival of a ship from Holland. On board was a letter for Governor Stuyvesant from the Dutch West India Company, giving the Jews their long-awaited permission to stay.

Freedom and Equality

Even though the Jews were now allowed to stay, Governor Stuyvesant put many limitations on their freedom. Jews could not travel to Fort Orange on the Hudson or down to the Delaware River to trade with the Native Americans—the main suppliers of beaver pelts, which were in great demand in Europe. There were restrictions, too, on the types of work Jews could do. In addition, the Jewish cemetery had to be outside the city walls.

The Dutch were in general a tolerant people. Since the Jews living in the Netherlands were free, they felt that the same freedom should be granted the Jews in the colonies. The Dutch West India Company, which had the final word, convinced Peter Stuyvesant and his Council of Nine to yield the right to travel to the Jews because of the need for experienced merchants and traders.

At first, Jews had also been forbidden to own their own homes, but they once again petitioned the Dutch West India Company, and this ban was also lifted.

When Stuyvesant organized an army to fight Swedish settlers to the south, the Jews were not allowed to join the army or stand guard at the city walls, though they were taxed for not standing guard. Once again, Asser Levy and Jacob Barsimson protested at city hall. Again the Dutch West India Company came to their defense and permitted them to stand guard at what is now Wall Street.

Asser Levy, now a prominent resident, longed to become a citizen of New Amsterdam and appeared before the council to apply. In 1657, his appeal was granted, and he became the first Jewish citizen of North America.

Daily Life

Most of the colonies in the New World were founded by groups, such as the Pilgrims in Massachusetts, looking for religious or political freedom. New Amsterdam, though, was a trading post of the Dutch West India Company. The first huts, wharves, and storehouses were built for use in the beaver trade with Native Americans along the Hudson River.

Because of this, the Dutch might have been more tolerant and friendly than other colonists. And, indeed, they helped the Jews adapt to life in New Amsterdam. The newcomers settled near what is now South William Street.

The Jewish women learned Dutch housekeeping and how to plant vegetable gardens and flower beds of Dutch bulbs, such as tulips and hyacinths. They also became skilled in knitting and sewing. Soon, they sat outside their homes exchanging gossip just as Dutch housewives did.

Jewish men traded with Native Americans and learned to fish from canoes.

Dutch homes were furnished with heavy mahogany, a style the Jews adopted. In general, the Jews welcomed the cheerful, unrestricted lifestyle of the Dutch.

Occupations

Asser Levy, a butcher by trade, opened a slaughterhouse outside the town wall at what is now Wall and Pearl Streets to prepare meat according to Jewish dietary laws. In the beginning, Jews were not allowed to own shops and stores or practice crafts. Since many were experienced traders, they were, however, allowed to trade with Europe, South America, the West Indies and other places in the world where they had family and friends. Trading was important to New Amsterdam since most necessities had to be brought in by ship from Europe and other places: Spinning wheels, oak storage chests, and the mahogany furniture, blue-and-white Dutch tiles, and even flower bulbs were shipped from Holland.

Jewish settlers were not allowed to own land or farm; so most remained in harbor cities

Jewish peddlers became important in the early colony, taking needed merchandise, such as coffee, sugar, and fabrics, to inland settlements and passing on to them news, culture, and bits of civilization. Traveling to remote areas along waterways or by horse and wagon over forest trails took courage and determination, but it was an important kind of employment for the Jews, whose past experience was mainly in trade and commerce, not physical labor. Later, some peddlers built crude wilderness huts to barter with the Native Americans, supplying them with beads, knives, axes, and cloth, in exchange for furs.

Spiritual Life

The spiritual life of the Jewish settlers was very important to them. While they adapted to the daily life of the Dutch, they kept their own religious traditions and holidays.

Governor Stuyvesant refused the Jews permission to build a synagogue, so they observed the Sabbath and religious festivals in their homes with other members of the Jewish community. All they needed were prayer shawls, the Torah, and a gathering of ten men. In 1655, six Jewish families came from Amsterdam, bringing with them the Torah, a scroll containing the five books of Moses.

The Jewish Cemetery

The first Jewish cemetery, consecrated in 1656, was outside the city walls, as decreed by Peter Stuyvesant, and there are no tombs remaining. Another Jewish cemetery, opened in 1682 on Chatham Square in lower New York, contains the graves of eighteen Jewish soldiers who fought in the American Revolution and also the graves of many of the early Jewish families.

The tombstone of Benjamin Bueno de Mesquita, buried in 1683, is the oldest still remaining. The first Jewish cantor—who conducted Jewish services in the early days—born in the Americas, Gershom Mendes Seixas, is also buried there.

The British Take Over

In 1664, the British took the colony of New Amsterdam from the Dutch. The British called the Jews "Portugals" and decided—since they were not Protestants governed by the state church of England—to let them take care of their own religious practices. The Jews finally were able to form a congregation, called Shearith Israel, and they rented a public hall for their religious services. By 1730, the first Jewish synagogue was built in New York. It was located on Mill Street, now South William Street.

In 1727, the General Assembly of New York voted that the words "on the true faith of a Christian" need not be included in the oath of citizenship. This event marked the beginning of the separation of church and state in the New World and allowed the Jews to become citizens.

Jews prospered under the British, and the community grew.

Glossary

Sephardim—Jews whose families originated in Spain or Portugal.

Marrano—The Spanish word for pig; it was applied to Jews who were forced to become Catholics in Spain. Their descendants were also called Marranos.

Inquisition—A court established by the Catholic Church to seek out Catholics who were not obeying Church laws. In Spain and Portugal the Inquisition was used against Marranos and others and did not hesitate to use torture or burning at the stake to make people say what the Inquisitors wanted.

Source Notes

Feingold, Henry L. *Zion in America: The Jewish Experience From Colonial Times to the Present*. New York: Hippocrene Books, Inc.

Goodman, Abram Vossen. *American Overture: Jewish Rights in Colonial Times*. Philadelphia: The Jewish Publication Society of America.

Grayzel, Solomon. *The History of the Jews: From the Babylonian Exile to the Establishment of Israel*. Philadelphia: The Jewish Publication Society of America.

Karp, Abraham J. *Haven and Home: A History of the Jews in America*. New York: Schocken Books.

Moscow, Henry. *The Street Book*. New York: The Hagstrom Map Company, Inc.

Pessin, Deborah. *History of the Jews in America*. New York: United Synagogue Commission on Jewish Education.

Tierney, Tom. *American Family of the Pilgrim Period*. New York: Dover Publications, Inc.

Warwick, Edward, Henry C. Pitz, Alexander Wyckoff. *Early American Dress*. New York: Benjamin Bloom.

Museum of the City of New York, New York City.

Index